This is about me, right here right now. I am sorry from the bottom of my heart, I have sat and thought where my actions and words have come from, my intent was never to cause you suffering in any form weather it was a one-time thing or a repeated action on my part over years. I am

sorry for not taking the

time to figure myself out

and to become someone

more capable to help, or to

act in certain situations to

be healthy for you and

everyone around me. I am

sorry, so causing myself

this suffering I learned a

great deal and am still

learning more and more

how to be the person I

know I deserve to be for the

ones that I love so dearly

and have previously

harmed with my words or

actions. I am sorry to them

and myself for not taking

the time to learn a new way

of operating for them and myself. I am growing and progressing in a lifestyle that is now healthier and more peaceful for all including, me.

Chapter 1

For-give

I forgive you for not taking
the time to unravel yourself
to see how you are
negatively affecting those
around you, including
yourself. I forgive you for
your words and your

actions that have created

chaos and harm to those

around you, and yourself. I

forgive you for being so

concerned with things

outside of yourself that you

never took the time to sit

with yourself to heal, so

that you can live a

healthier and more

peaceful lifestyle. I forgive you for the times you brought only stress, troubles and chaos. I forgive you, and I forgive myself for allowing this in my life. I forgive myself for not acknowledging my own worth that I deserve peace and a healthy lifestyle. I forgive myself for not

knowing what I did not

know, but now I can see

better that I deserve peace,

I deserve the space to grow

a healthy lifestyle.

I am sorry for you and

myself for not knowing, I

forgive you and myself for

all harms caused and

allowed. I now know I am

worthy and deserving of a

peaceful life and any

other's stress or unpeaceful

ways are no longer my

weight to carry. I forgive

you, for now I see this

weight you brought was

never mine to carry, the

resentments and anger I

had towards you was never

because of you it was

because I took them on

because I care for you. I

still car for you a great

deal, and always will. I can

see now that I can love you

while still hoping you only

the best and that you

continue to choose a

healthier more peaceful life.

Forgiving someone who

isn't sorry. At this moment

to forgive them is not

saying what they have done

or are doing is right, but to

simply acknowledge that what they are doing or how they are acting is not who they are. Forgive, definition is to stop feeling angry or resentful towards (someone) for an offense, flaw or mistake. To forgive someone you are freeing yourself of the feelings of anger and resentment. You are saying you see they are suffering within the decisions they make. You are making new boundaries for those you must learn to love at a distance and simply saying I let go of all actions, words, or flaws of (this person). You are saying, 'I am ridding myself of these feeling towards this suffering person, I am freeing myself of any negative feeling towards them so that I can live more peacefully.' Then create internal boundaries of how to love them while keeping a distance that is safe for you from them in their words, actions or flaws.

By forgiving you are giving up all the negative feeling you have towards someone and you are allowing yourself the space to move forward in a healthier

lifestyle.

"Forgive others, not because they deserve forgiveness, but because you deserve peace."

-Johnathan Lockwood Huie

Chapter 2

The Boundaries.

Forgive them and keep them forgiven.

We forgive. Then we forget.

Well in a sense yes.

Forgive, let go of all the

details of the reason you

needed to forgive this

person. That's a lot of mental space you can fill with something positive! But, do not forget that this is someone who has hurt you, most likely because they them selves are suffering and have not taken the time to understand themselves.

What I mean by that is

Forgive them and forget the

reason you were upset, but

do not forget that you have

boundaries in place now for

a reason, to protect

yourself! To protect your

mental peace, to protect

your progression into a

healthier lifestyle.

Whether these new

boundaries are that they

can no longer come over,

and you no longer want to

go ever to visit them, but

you are comfortable

meeting them out to eat.

That is your boundary. Or

if you only wish to

encounter them now in a

group or with another

person there. That is your

boundary. If you choose to

not share pictures or your

social media with this

person. That is your

boundary. Whatever you

feel necessary for you to

maintain and grow into a

more peaceful healthy way

22

of life. You do, and no not

forget that.

Forgiving is not about the

other person, it is about

you. It is about putting the

weight of resentment and

anger down that you had

towards this person.

Setting boundaries to protect yourself from their stresses or anxieties that arise from interacting with them, and moving forward with your life in a healthier, more positive, progressive way. Forgetting the negativity and remembering if this person is to remain

in your life that you have a
reason for your boundaries.

Maintaining your
boundaries, maybe the
factor that allows you to
maintain any sort of
relationship with this
person. If this is someone

you greatly care for, by you learning how to maintain healthy boundaries will most likely be the factor that permits this person to still be (as you allow) in your life. If they are too toxic for your life, moving on completely may be the best of all decisions.

"Resentment is

like drinking

poison, and then

hoping it will kill

your enemies."

-Nelson Mendela

Chapter 3

So now what?

Having forgiven someone and creating your safe boundaries of how you will allow interaction with them into your life, and now moving forward. They may ask why you are distant, they may think you have changed, they may question your new approach to how you choose to interact with them. I suggest simply saying, I'm on a journey to a more peaceful and progressive life, my time has just been fuller of choosing and learning a

healthy lifestyle. Or another

thing I have said is, 'would

you like to read with me?'

Because I have changed a

lot, that was the point. I

Took a negatively filled

spike out of my back,

forgave and gave up all the

weight that spike was

holding, and am learning a healthier way of operating for myself.

It is ok if they don't understand, and it is ok if people think you are acting different. The point is this is for you, for you to live in peace, and grow a healthier, less of stress

lifestyle.

Encouraging others to grow

and do the same is fine, for

me I find sharing my

excitement and relief of new

positive ways of thinking or

living has inspired others to

explore for themselves.

Being the change we wish

to see, is more effective

than I ever realized... until I

started to do just that.

Walk forward in your new

developed healthy

boundaries. Forgiving those

around you and yourself for

not knowing what you did

not know, and them for not

knowing what they did not

know. Seeing the suffering

caused to themselves and

to yourself, create your

clear boundaries and see

how things most likely

begin to change for more

peace in your life.

34

For more life learning inspiration:

Instagram: @_Just.b___

Facebook: @just.b.llc

YouTube: Britney Anne

YouTube: Just.b The Island

Always all the best with

love,

-Britney Anne Klump